Truck
Trouble

FIRST EDITION
Editors Jennifer Siklós and Caroline Bingham; **Designer** Michelle Baxter;
Senior Editor Linda Esposito; **Deputy Managing Art Editor** Jane Horne; **US Editor** Regina Kahney;
Pre-Production Producer Nadine King; **Producer** Sara Hu; **Photography** Richard Leeney;
Reading Consultant Linda Gambrell, PhD

THIS EDITION
Editorial Management by Oriel Square
Produced for DK by WonderLab Group LLC
Jennifer Emmett, Erica Green, Kate Hale, *Founders*

Editors Grace Hill Smith, Libby Romero, Michaela Weglinski;
Photography Editors Kelley Miller, Annette Kiesow, Nicole DiMella;
Managing Editor Rachel Houghton; **Designers** Project Design Company; **Researcher** Michelle Harris;
Copy Editor Lori Merritt; **Indexer** Connie Binder; **Proofreader** Larry Shea;
Reading Specialist Dr. Jennifer Albro; **Curriculum Specialist** Elaine Larson

Published in the United States by DK Publishing
1745 Broadway, 20th Floor, New York, NY 10019

Copyright © 2023 Dorling Kindersley Limited
DK, a Division of Penguin Random House LLC
23 24 25 26 27 10 9 8 7 6 5 4 3 2 1
001–333432–Apr/2023

All rights reserved.
Without limiting the rights under the copyright reserved
above, no part of this publication may be reproduced, stored
in or introduced into a retrieval system, or transmitted, in any
form, or by any means (electronic, mechanical, photocopying,
recording, or otherwise), without the prior written permission
of the copyright owner.
Published in Great Britain by Dorling Kindersley Limited

A catalog record for this book
is available from the Library of Congress.
HC ISBN: 978-0-7440-6700-2
PB ISBN: 978-0-7440-6701-9

DK books are available at special discounts when purchased
in bulk for sales promotions, premiums, fundraising, or
educational use. For details, contact: DK Publishing Special Markets,
1745 Broadway, 20th Floor, New York, NY 10019
SpecialSales@dk.com

Printed and bound in China

The publisher would like to thank the following for their kind permission to reproduce their images:
a=above; c=center; b=below; l=left; r=right; t=top; b/g=background
Alamy Stock Photo: Viktoriia Novokhatska 23clb; **Dreamstime.com:** Smontgom65 26tr, 30clb;
Shutterstock.com: beeboys 15cra, Gorodenkoff 12c, Johnny Habell 4-5, Olga Miltsova 14clb
Cover images: *Front:* **Shutterstock.com:** johnpluto; *Back:* **Dreamstime.com:** Manatchaya Suratanachaikul cla;
Shutterstock.com: Ivan Lukyanchuk cra, pingebat clb
All other images © Dorling Kindersley

For the curious
www.dk.com

Truck
Trouble

Angela Royston

Contents

6 Getting Ready

16 Trouble Ahead

26 Special Delivery

30 Glossary
31 Index
32 Quiz

Getting Ready

John got up very early to make a special delivery. He climbed up two steps into his big, blue truck.

7

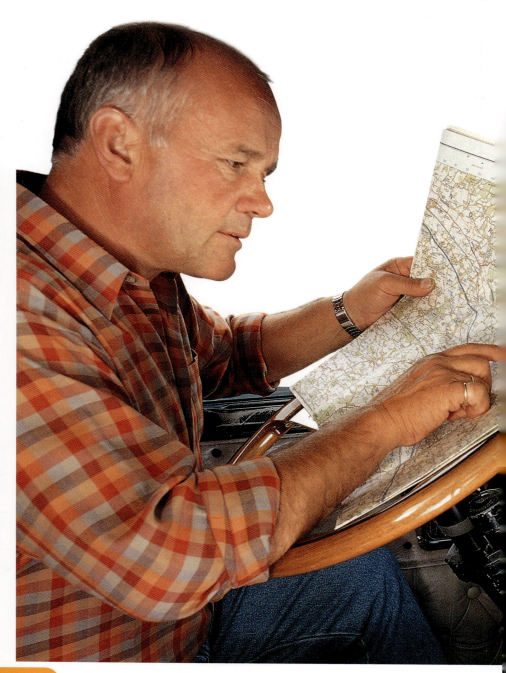

John looked at the map. Today was no day to get lost! Then, he started the truck, checked the mirrors, and set off.

mirror

At a service station, John checked the engine. It needed some oil. Then, he filled up the fuel tank.

fuel tank

He looked at the shiny engine. "Don't let me down!" he said. "I can't be late!"

11

Next, he had to pick up the cargo. A forklift raised big boxes into the back of John's truck.

warehouse workers

forklift

There were also some small boxes marked "Special Delivery." John put these in the truck, too.

John was in a hurry, but he was also very hungry. He pulled into a truck stop for breakfast.

breakfast

John's friend Anita arrived in her milk tanker. She joined John for breakfast. Then, she left for work.

milk tanker

Trouble Ahead

After breakfast, John drove to the factory.

He waved to the workers as he drove in.
They helped him unload the big boxes.

"I'm in a hurry," John told them.
"I've got another delivery to make."
Soon, he was on his way.
But there was trouble ahead.

A van had broken down!
John slammed on
his brakes.
His truck screeched
to a halt.

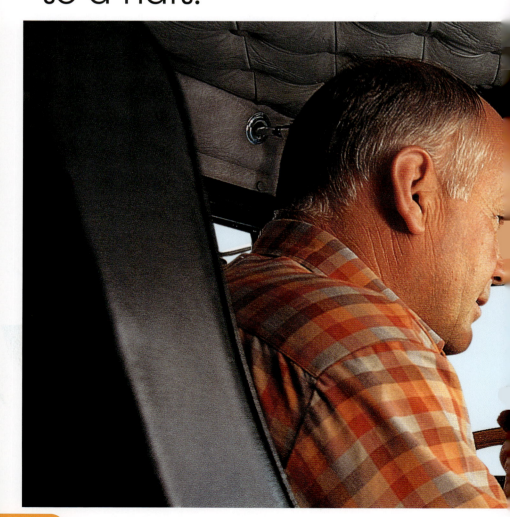

The road was very narrow.
John's truck was too wide to get past the van.

John used his radio to call for help.
He also warned all other drivers to stay away from that road.

Soon, John saw flashing lights.
It was a tow truck!
The truck towed the van to a garage.

When the road was clear, John hurried on his way. But there was more trouble ahead!

Boom! Boom!

John drove into a thunderstorm. Rain began to pour down.

John turned on the windshield wipers.

He drove very slowly. "This isn't my day!" he groaned.

wiper

BANG!

"Oh no! A flat tire!" John grabbed his tools and the spare wheel.

bolt

He unscrewed the bolts and took off the wheel. Then, he put on the spare. It was hard work!

Special Delivery

John drove into town.
He had to wait for the traffic light to turn green.

traffic light

"Hurry up!" thought John.
He was almost late
for his special delivery.
At last, John arrived.

There was no time
to spare!
He unloaded the boxes
marked "Special Delivery."

John was just in time for the party at the new children's hospital.

Inside the special boxes were piles of toys.
"Thank you!" shouted the children.
"It was no trouble!" said John.

Glossary

bolt
a screw without a sharp point used to fasten things

fuel tank
a large container for storing fuel

mirror
a piece of glass that helps to see what's behind you

traffic lights
a row of colored lights that control traffic

wiper
a long, thin tool that wipes away water

Index

bolts 24

boxes 12, 13, 17, 27, 29

brakes 18

cargo 12

engine 11

flat tire 24

forklift 12

fuel tank 11

map 9

milk tanker 15

mirror 9

oil 11

radio 20

service station 11

tow truck 21

toys 29

traffic light 26

truck 6, 9, 12, 13, 18, 19

truck stop 14

van 18, 19, 21

wheel 24

wipers 23

Quiz

Answer the questions to see what you have learned. Check your answers with an adult.

1. What vehicle did a worker use to raise the big boxes into John's truck?
2. Where did John deliver the big boxes?
3. What vehicle arrived to help the broken-down van?
4. When John's truck got a flat tire, what did he unscrew to take off the wheel?
5. What was inside the boxes marked "Special Delivery"?

1. A forklift 2. A factory 3. A tow truck 4. Bolts
5. Toys for children